FAIRY GARDEN

HANDBOOK

LIZA GARDNER WALSH

FAIRY GARDEN
ᚷHANDBOOKᚷ

Down East

ISBN 978-1-60893-214-6

Design by Lynda Chilton

Printed in China

5   4   3   2   1

BOOKS·MAGAZINE·ONLINE
www.downeast.com

Distributed to the trade by National Book Network

Library of Congress Cataloging-in-Publication Data:

Walsh, Liza Gardner.
 Fairy garden handbook / by Liza Gardner Walsh. -- 1st ed.
    p. cm.
 ISBN 978-1-60893-214-6 (trade hardcover : alk. paper)
1. Gardens, Miniature. 2. Gardening for children. 3. Miniature decorative design. 4. Garden ornaments and furniture. 5. Nature craft. I. Title.
 SB433.5W353 2013
 635.083--dc23
                          2012043271

*To my mom, Barbara Gardner,
the master gardener who showed
me how to grow.*

*And always to Phoebe and Daphne,
my flower fairies, who take such
good care of the world.*

Contents

Introduction ~ 9

1 Getting Started ~ 13
Sun; Soil; Food; Water; Tools

2 Container Fairy Gardens ~ 21
*Containers; Plants; Planting and Hardscaping; Accessories;
An Interview with Kerri Day*

3 Outdoor Fairy Gardens ~ 37
*Plants; Flowers with a Fairy Purpose;
Flowers for Fairy Potions and Protection; Accessories*

4 Garden Projects ~ 49
*Butterfly Gardens; Birds in the Garden;
Scent Gardens; Garden Forts; Music and Light*

5 Fairy Garden Tea Party ~ 61
Invitations; Planning; Menus; Activities

6 Indoor Projects ~ 69
*Indoor Fairy Gardens; Pressed Flowers;
Bulbs; Pocket Plots*

**7 How to Know if Fairies
Have Visited Your Garden ~ 75**

Further Reading ~ 79

Resources ~ 81

Acknowledgements ~ 83

Introduction

"Garden fairies come at dawn. Bless the flowers and then they're gone."

Welcome to the garden — a place where a seed as small as a grain of sand transforms into a dazzling flower. Wherever such magic exists, you can bet fairies will be near. People say that when a seed sprouts, a fairy baby is born. In fact, there's an entire fleet of fairies devoted solely to flowers. Mary Cicely Barker, the flower fairy godmother, reports the following about flower fairies:

"A flower fairy's job is to look after her plant, tending leaves and trimming flowers. A flower fairy is 2–4 inches tall, and has a pair of delicate wings. She dresses in the leaves and flowers from her plant to help her stay hidden. A flower fairy is not at all fussy about where she lives: hanging baskets, window boxes, a tiny crack in a crumbling wall, or between the pavement stones where weeds and mosses grow — any of these places might be home to a flower fairy. Since almost everyone has a potted plant, or can see a patch of grass or treetops from their window, this means that almost everyone is close to a flower fairy even if they don't realize it at the time." (From *My Garden of Flower Fairies*)

Perhaps you have already seen a fairy or made multiple houses in the woods for them, now is your chance to make them a garden. You may ask, what is fairy gardening, and that is a good question. Fairy gardening is simply gardening with the fairies in mind. For example, planting flowers that fairies might use for clothing or to bring to the fairy queen on the first of May. Or you might make a tiny trellis for a miniature landscape or a bench for a mossy container garden. There are many types of fairy gardens and many possibilities for the fairy gardener due to the vast

number of plants available. There are fairy gardens that also attract hummingbirds and butterflies, friends of the fairies, or gardens filled with wonderful scents that will delight a fairy's sense of smell. A fairy garden can be grown in your yard or planted in containers, such as wheelbarrows, bathtubs, baskets, or plain old pots.

When building a fairy house, the most important rule is to use only natural materials. To bring a bunch of man-made items into the woods is basically littering. Since a fairy garden is either in a container or in a cultivated garden, you are allowed to bring on the shimmer, the sparkle, the tiny watering cans. But now that you have this freedom, don't go crazy. Fairies still prefer natural materials, even in a garden. Always think whether a fairy would really appreciate that extra marble or if it just makes the garden look too cluttered. **The most important rule as you begin your entry into the magical world of fairy gardening is to never use any chemical fertilizers or pesticides and to always garden organically.** By planting a fairy garden, you are being trusted by the fairies to be a guardian of nature and anyone who is a steward of the environment will earn their blessing.

Some of you may remember when you built your very first fairy house and knew by instinct exactly how to create one. I bet you will have the same feeling with your fairy garden once you get a couple of gardening techniques down. Plus, you will probably have amazing ideas like my friend Ian, who wanted to make a beetle stable in his fairy garden because the fairies like to get rides from beetles. The possibilities are limitless.

This book is for anyone, even if the only thing you've ever made in the garden is a mud pie (there are actually two sections that rely on mud pies)! It is filled with projects and ideas for you, your family, and friends to make your yard, porch, or windowsill a welcome landing pad for fairies. We will cover some of the basics about how to garden because there is a lot you can learn about this activity. People spend lifetimes perfecting their plots. But you are starting young and enlisting the fairies' help, which is a guaranteed recipe for success. As you enter this magical domain, listen for the fairies. Listen as they share their all-important fairy code. It will make you a better gardener and person: "Be careful, neat, polite, friendly, humorous, generous, honest, kind, and work hard." Oh, and don't forget to laugh. I mean it! Fairies love laughter.

Getting Started

*"I'll seek a four-leaved shamrock in all
thy fairy dells, And if I find the charmed leaves,
oh, how I'll weave my spells!"*

~ SAMUEL LOVER

Even if the only seed you have ever planted was a sunflower seed that happened to fall out of your trail mix, you can easily learn to garden. This chapter will cover the basics of what a plant needs to survive. Believe it or not, plants are a lot like you. They need sun, water, food, and soil. Okay, so *you* don't necessarily *need* soil. We will get into some specific types of gardening later, like fairy container gardens and butterfly gardens, but for now this is Gardening 101.

SUN

Every plant needs the sun, but some need it more and others less. Plants can be shade loving or sun loving, vital information when choosing plants for your garden. Before you put a garden in the ground, take a good look around your yard. You can even draw a map. Gardens under trees will be shady, but maybe there is a spot in your backyard that gets afternoon sun and is tucked away in a nice private spot next to a big rock. Perfect. But before you start digging, watch your future garden site carefully. Check it in the morning — is it sunny? Lunchtime? 3:00? Dinnertime? You can even start a little garden journal to record your observations. Once you are satisfied with the amount of light that this spot gets each day, you have an official garden plot. In this very spot you will now get to look even deeper. Now, get ready to dig!

SOIL

We all know plants don't grow out of thin air. They grow in soil, which is just another word for dirt. And when you garden there is no escaping getting a little dirty. If the thought of tunneling your hands deep into a pile of dirt does not appeal to you, then now is the time to find yourself a pair of nice gardening gloves. But, if you are like me and love to burrow right in, this next exercise will be right up your alley. This is loosely called the "Mud Pie Approach to Soil Identification." Grab a shovel and dig at least six inches in your garden site. Grab a handful of dirt and squeeze it as hard as you can. If it stays together, you have clay soil. If it falls apart, you have sandy soil. But, if it stays together until you touch it, then you have loam. Loam is the golden ticket, it is light and fluffy, allowing water and food to easily reach the plant, but firm enough to hold down roots. If you find that your soil is not of the loamy variety, no problem. By adding compost and peat moss and giving your soil a good mixing with a shovel or hoe, you will most likely improve your soil. For those of you with a scientific bent who really want to investigate, you can send a sample of your soil to the local 4-H group in your community. They will send it back with a description of the composition of your soil. You will get into all kinds of fancy stuff like the levels of acid and alkaline.

FOOD

Back to compost, a.k.a. dinnertime for the garden. Compost is broken-down organic matter. If you are going to really pursue gardening, then I highly recommend that you begin your own compost pile. This is a great family project that will save a ton of garbage from entering the landfill. All of your parents' coffee grounds, the egg shells from breakfast, and all of the peelings from your carrots will now return to the ground and break down, forming nutrients for your garden. The fairies will applaud you for this because composting makes your plants healthier and you'll get an environmental A+.

There is another type of food that gardens love. Manure. Yes, you might also know it as poop. Go ahead and giggle, but manure is no laughing matter when it comes to making a healthy garden. And you don't even need very much, just a scoop of poop will do.

Healthy soil is home to worms. If when you are digging, no little worms wriggle away from your fingers, then you really should find some to add to your soil. Worms make the soil breathable for plants. To use a fancy word, they aerate it. Well-aerated soil allows your plants to get all the nutrients they need to thrive. So, next time you go fishing and buy some worms, save half for your garden.

WATER

Now, for the star of the show, water, glorious water. No plant can live without good old H_2O, but similar to the way some plants prefer sun and others prefer shade, some plants are thirstier than

others. Generally, too much water will make mud soup and drown your plants, and too little will create a drought, making your garden look like the Sahara Desert. I have found two easy tests to make sure you get it just right. The first is called the stone test. When you plant your garden or container, put a good-size stone right on top of it. Every couple of days, lift the stone up and look at the bottom. If it is damp, no need to water. If it is dry, get out the watering can. The other trick is really simple. Take your index finger and stick it into the soil at least two inches. If it is dry down there, then you need to water. Sometimes a garden seems perfectly watered but is only wet on the surface. One of the most important times to water is when something is first planted. Plants get stressed out when they move from their tiny little pots into a whole new place and water eases their transition.

TOOLS

If you have figured out sun, soil, water, and food, then you are well on your way to master gardening. But in addition to those essentials, there are some tools that will help you really dig. A small **hand trowel** is essential for planting, and a garden fork helps pull up weedy patches in your garden. If you want to remember what plants you planted, **plant markers** are useful. You can buy these at a garden store or just recycle your leftover Popsicle sticks — yum! A good **watering can** and a spray bottle are essential to keep your plants from getting too thirsty. A **wheelbarrow** is a garden workhorse that makes lugging dirt around the garden

much easier, plus it's fun to get a ride from your parents sometimes. As I mentioned before, if you don't like getting your hands dirty or if a cat has made your garden a frequent potty stop, **gloves** are a good idea. And **boots** never hurt, especially during mud season.

But truly, the only tools that the fairies want you to have are not the things you can buy at the garden store. The first is a respect for all the life of the garden. Be gentle with your plants and kind to the tiny creatures who visit them. Use only organic and natural materials. I'll say it again, a fairy will never visit a yard that has been sprayed with chemicals. But most importantly, have fun digging, planting, and watching your garden bloom.

Container Gardens

*"Hand in hand with fairy grace
will we sing and bless this place."*

~ WILLIAM SHAKESPEARE

The best way to get started in this fairy gardening business is to start small. A container garden allows you to make a tiny world for a fairy while requiring only a few plants and accessories. There are some tricks to working with a container, which we will cover, but the key is that it's portable. If you visit your grandparents, you can stick your fairy garden in the car. Of course, if you choose to build a fairy garden in an old bathtub, mobility will not be an option. The

container garden is also the best choice for those budding fairy gardeners who live in cities and have small backyards. Keep in mind that container gardens are very sensitive to wind and need protection from the elements.

CONTAINERS

The first step in creating a fairy container garden is to pick the container. There are so many choices here, and few limitations. Old wheelbarrows, straw hats, ice buckets, your very own red wagon, baskets, and plain old-fashioned terracotta planters will all work as long as the container is deep enough to allow at least three inches of dirt so the roots of the plants can spread. The other essential consideration with a container is drainage. Ideally, there should be a few drainage holes that are standard in most gardening pots. If there are no holes because you have gone with the wheelbarrow option, you will first need to line the bottom with gravel or the broken shards of a terracotta pot.

If choosing a basket, make sure it is lined with a garbage bag with some holes poked through to avoid rot.

Once the drainage solution is reached to prevent soggy, moldy roots, add your soil. For most types of fairy gardens a standard soil recipe is two parts commercial soil, one part peat moss or compost. Never use soil excavated from your outside garden as container plants are pickier and that dirt might be prone to weeds. Fill the container halfway with the soil mixture and get ready to plant.

PLANTS

A container garden relies on the use of miniature and dwarf plants. There are thousands of beautiful plants in the world, but for your fairy container garden choose those that thrive in a container and will make a fairy want to visit. The following are just a few of the more common choices to get you started.

Myrtle: The variegated (different colored patterns on the leaves) or green variety can be shaped into a small tree.

Lemon-scented Geranium: Smells delicious and can also be trimmed into a tree shape. This is only one of the many types of scented geraniums available.

Creeping Savory: Can be shaped into a small bush or allowed to trail down the side of your container.

Irene Rosemary: This is cascading rosemary that drapes over the side of your container. Rosemary will entice the fairies to visit your garden.

Oregano: Tiny pink flowers look like a miniature flower bush and oregano is great in pasta sauce!

Sage: Gray and variegated leaves make a nice contrast to the other plants in your container.

Irish and Scotch Moss: Moss is essential as it provides the perfect bed for a fairy.

CHIVES

MOSS

OREGANO

BABY'S TEARS

❀ **Baby's Tears:** With their tiny leaves and ability to cluster as well as cascade, this is a perfect plant for small spaces.

❀ **Chives:** Chives can be trimmed so they look like a hedge. The clippings are great in your favorite salad! (You like salad, right?)

The trick for figuring out the right plants is to look at your container and determine if you have enough room. For an average-size planter, say ten inches across, I recommend choosing three or four plants. But make sure they all have the same light, soil, and water requirements. Remember this essential gardening adage, "right plant, right place." While your plants are still in their pots, try placing them in different spots

on top of the soil in your container. This way you'll know right where you want them to go before you start planting. If you have a trailing plant like Irene rosemary, then it should be planted close to the edge. Place the tallest plant in the middle. Also, think about where a fairy could get forty winks or find a hidden spot.

I always recommend drawing a plan, even for your tiny container garden. Take a blank piece of paper and a black pen and draw the outline of your container. Where do you want your plants? Do you envision pathways, hills, or a river? Drawing your plan also gives you a break, allowing you to imagine all of the fairy garden possibilities. Write a little wish on the corner of your plan for a fairy to help make your garden thrive.

PLANTING AND HARDSCAPING

When you've decided where everything is going to go, gently squeeze the plant from its pot. Take a look at the roots. Are they a thick block of tangled white mess? This means the plant is root bound and it happens when plants grow fast in a small pot. They are so happy you have freed them! If you have a root-bound plant, simply pinch off the end of the thickest part of the root. If they are only a little root bound, gently tease apart the roots. Dig a hole for your plant, set the plant in, and cover gently with dirt. Finally, give those little guys a drink. It's stressful moving so much! But be gentle and use a small watering can. Pat down the wet dirt to prepare for the next phase in your design.

You have created the foundation of your fairy garden. Next is the really fun part where a few plants turn into a shimmering fairyland. Pathways, a pond, a bridge; these are just some of the structural elements you can now build. Sand out-lined by shiny marbles or sea glass makes a distinctive pathway. A small empty plastic container buried in the dirt makes an ideal pond. The hardscaping, which is what this building stage is called, should all be created before you begin to add your accessories.

ACCESSORIES

Who can resist a miniature wheelbarrow or a watering can no bigger than your thumb? How about a garden bench the size of your baby sister's foot? Not me, and probably very few fairies. But listen, don't go crazy spending all of your allowance and tooth fairy money on tiny garden things when chances are you're an expert at building and creating. Remember all those pieces of furniture you made for your fairy house. The table made from a thin rock held up by four sticks stuck in the ground. The baby cradle made out of a mussel shell lined with corn silk. Fairy gardens allow you the same opportunity to make natural elements into fairy furniture. And I believe that fairies would rather sit on a chair made from something natural than one made of plastic.

This is the time to pull out your collections. Sea shells can serve in fairy gardens as bathtubs, birdbaths, and seats. Periwinkles make tidy borders for small ponds. And don't forget your precious sea glass, fairy gardens are made for sea glass embellishment! While creating your fairy landscape, think about the fairies. Remember how they love privacy, so make sure there are hidden areas where they can take cover. And they love taking naps, so give them a soft cushion to rest their wings on. And is there a special table where you can set gifts of milk and marbles? But most importantly, seriously, you must laugh when planting your garden. Fairies love the laughter of children, and there is nothing that will guarantee more fairy visitations than a garden created with delight.

An interview with fairy garden expert and accessory maker Kerri Day

WHY DO YOU LOVE CREATING MINIATURE GARDENS FOR FAIRIES?

I've always loved small things and gardening. So, this is a way to combine the two. I'm like a kid when I am working on them. The other amazing thing is that everyone in our family, even the neighbors' kid, enjoys creating them.

DO YOU HAVE ANY GOOD STORIES ABOUT FAIRIES IN THE GARDEN?

I've never seen a fairy, but I do see a little girl who loves every aspect of creating a place for them to visit each year. From the walks with Dad in the woods or gravel pit to find special items, to the "cleaning the grounds" with Mom and setting up the new year's place, to the "show and tell" of all who come to visit us after.

WHAT DO YOU THINK IS THE FAIRIES' FAVORITE ACCESSORY THAT YOU MAKE?

I love gnomes, and my favorite creations are ones with the cement tables embossed with leaves, chairs made of wood and birch bark, plates and cups created from nature's wood as well, with one of my gnomes standing near. They are the perfect size.

WHAT IS YOUR FAVORITE ACCESSORY?

I think that fairies love shiny things, so my favorite item to add at the end of a creation is a marble in just the right color, in just the right spot, and if it is not a marble, it's a shiny glass droplet.

WHAT ARE SOME OF THE BEST PLANTS FOR A CONTAINER GARDEN?

For tall items I use houseplants, something from the fern family. You can easily divide them to use only what looks good. Then there are plenty of miniature perennials and annuals you can find. Just remember that they do grow, and think about the size they will end up becoming. Again, you can divide them up and start small, knowing they will continue to grow. I do have one other secret: I have a couple of ways that I can miniaturize hosta. They will stay small for the first year. The hostas are my favorite!

Outdoor Fairy Gardens

Each fairy breath of summer, as it blows
with loveliness, inspires the blushing rose.

~ AUTHOR UNKNOWN

Now that you know the basics of gardening — sun, soil, food, and water — and have perhaps planted your own miniature fairy garden, get ready to head into the wilds of your backyard. The question is where do you want to put this fairy garden? If you have a small yard or garden, the decision will be made simply out of the process of elimination. If your parents are avid gardeners and every inch of your yard is planted, this makes your choice trickier. Maybe despite all of the plantings, there is one bare spot beneath a group of tall plants. Ask your parents if you can "fair-ify" this place. To fair-ify means adding a fairy element and maybe even a few plants that attract the fairies. A fairy house is a great example of "fair-ification."

If you are able to make a brand new garden bed, then onward, ho! Remember how we talked about the sun and mapping out a garden spot in Chapter 1? Now is the time to look for a quiet spot in the garden that gets a good amount of sun. If the site has a natural feature nearby, such as a rock or a stump, or a creek running beside it — bonus! You just need a good patch of earth that your parents say is okay for you to carve up. Once you've designated your garden site, think about the shape you might like; rectangle, circle, or even a spiral. Again, draw a plan before you begin to dig, then get out those indispensible tools and start to excavate. If you are removing grass, be especially thorough in getting it out because if you miss too much, your garden will be plagued by weeds for years. Once you have cleared the site, amend the soil with good old compost and peat moss and get ready to plant.

PLANTS

The choices for the outdoor garden are much broader than those for your container garden, but there are a couple of factors to consider. First, there are two main types of plants: perennials and annuals. Perennials come back every year, whereas annuals only last one season. Gardeners often add annuals to established beds and containers to provide bursts of color, but perennials are the real backbone of a garden. Second, hold on to that great saying, "right

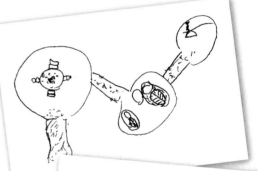

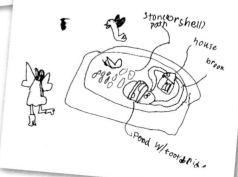

NASTURTIUMS

POPPY

DELPHINIUM

DOWNY WOODMINT

CHINESE LANTERNS

plant, right place," when picking out your plants. A plant meant for shade will wilt in full sun.

Did you know that learning the meaning of flowers is akin to learning fairy language? By placing certain combinations of the flowers that fairies covet in your garden, you are inviting them to visit and are actually speaking to them. Not every flower has a specific fairy use or definition, but it's hard for you to go wrong since most flowers are sure to make a fairy happy. There is one flower, though, that will repel a fairy as quick as a blink and that is St. John's wort. The number one fairy favorite is the bluebell. They eat them, they make music with the bells, they make hats for their babies, and they generally adore them. If you only grow one thing in your garden to attract fairies, this is the plant. The following is a list of some of the plants that fairies have a special relationship to. Renowned fairy garden expert and enthusiast Betty Earl compiled many of the following in her book, *Fairy Gardens: A Guide to Growing an Enchanted Miniature World.*

FLOWERS WITH A FAIRY PURPOSE

❀ **Thyme:** The perfect plant for cushions and soft fairy beds.

❀ **Nasturtiums:** Fairy umbrellas and platters for feasts.

❀ **Any Bell-shaped Flowers (Lily of the valley, coral bells, bluebells):** Can be used to create fairy music, hats, and dresses.

Lavender: Important for fairy laundry.

Chinese Lanterns: The flowers look like lanterns and light the way for fairy gatherings.

Ferns: The fronds of ferns make perfect blankets.

Lady's Mantle: The dew drops that pour off this plant give the fairies a place to shower.

Hollyhocks: The flowers are made into dancing skirts.

4-O'clocks: Fairies use these as a timepiece since they bloom in the afternoon.

Lamb's Ear: This soft, fuzzy leaf is the perfect blanket.

Queen Anne's Lace: This lacy blossom is perfect for curtains, coverlets, and lacy shawls.

Fairy Duster: Just as the name implies, this plant makes a great fairy broom.

Snapdragons: Fairies use these as puppets.

Milkweed Pods: In the fall, fairies use the dried husks filled with downy seeds as cradles.

FERN

LADY'S MANTLE

HOLLYHOCKS

LAMB'S EAR

QUEEN ANNES LACE

LILAC

TULIP

COWSLIPS

DAISY

FOREGET-ME-NOT

BLUEBELL

CLOVER

🌸 **Elderberry:** Berries and blossoms from this plant are used to make fairy wine.

🌸 **Rose and Lilac:** The fragrances of these plants draw fairies to your garden.

FLOWERS FOR FAIRY POTIONS AND PROTECTION:

🌸 **Tulips:** Symbolize loyalty, which is a very important trait for fairies.

🌸 **Violets:** A favorite of the fairy queen and used in many celebrations.

🌸 **Primrose:** This plant makes fairies invisible to humans.

🌸 **Apple Blossoms:** Used by fairies as a doorway into a human garden.

🌸 **Cowslips:** Help humans in their quests for fairy gold.

🌸 **Daisy:** Being in a field of daisies can allow you to see fairies, but wearing a daisy chain will keep children safe from mischievous fairies.

🌸 **Forget-me-not:** The tiny blossoms of this flower uncover fairy mysteries.

🌸 **Gardenia:** This flower allows fairies to protect children.

Harebell: The flowers of this plant are said to help you see fairies.

Clover: A sacred fairy plant even though many gardeners consider this plant a weed.

Marigold: If you collect the dew from the leaves of a marigold and rub it around your eyes, you may see a fairy. But be very careful with anything that you put near your eyes.

Pansy: Powerful love potions are made by fairies from the petals of the pansy.

Peony: If you place peonies in a vase next to your bed at night, you will dream of fairies.

Heather: This plant helps open the door between the fairy realm and our world. It also brings gentle fairies to your garden if you make a bouquet on May 1 and leave it out as an offering for the fairies.

MARIGOLD

PANSY

ROSE

HEATHER

This is a lot of information and if you feel overwhelmed, don't worry. Pick three of the flowers you recognize and start there. Buying several seed packets, such as nasturtiums and marigolds, makes the endeavor more affordable. Put together a list of plants you must have this year and start planting those. Next year, add three more. Gardens take time, patience, and the ability to try new things. Before you know it, you will be speaking the language of flowers.

ACCESSORIES

Once you've chosen your plants and readied the soil for their entrance into the garden, step back and prepare, as I said earlier, to "fair-ify" your garden. Other than the plants, accessories are the most important part of making a garden a fairy garden! As with the container garden, you can spend a lot of money and buy a bunch of premade items or you can use that amazing noggin of yours to create your own fairy garden furnishings and accessories. Here are a few items that are easy to make and add a lot of panache to your garden site.

The whole reason you made this garden is so fairies will visit, so one of the first things you should do is make a **welcome sign**. Your sign can be simple or complex, but one way to do it is to find a piece of driftwood or birch bark and write "Welcome" with a permanent marker. Then glue the sign between two sticks and set it in the garden for all the fairies to see. For an industrious version of this endeavor, glue tiny pebbles or shells into the shape of the letters.

43

A fairy house is a great addition to your garden and, as you may well know, fairies love it when someone offers them a home. There are entire books written about this subject (hint, hint), and the possibilities for building are endless. When building a fairy house in your garden, make sure it is scaled correctly for the area you are working in, and make sure it blends in with the plants and other garden features.

Fairy doors are a symbol of the portal (fancy word for gateway) between our world and theirs. And they look really cute. Do fairies really open and close these doors? Good question, but they are simple to make out of bark with a tiny acorn or a berry glued on for a knob. Or you can glue a bunch of sticks that are all the same size together into a larger rectangle and then attach a sea-shell knob. There are beautiful examples of artisan-made fairy doors on the Internet and in many fairy-themed boutiques if you wish to go shopping.

If you are not up for the task of making a fairy door, **an arbor** performs a similar portal function. A very talented fairy gardener who I know made a pussy willow arbor by braiding three pussy willow vines and bending them into an arch. The pussy willows are so soft and sweet that any fairy would be crazy not to enter.

Another fairy garden essential is **a trellis**. A trellis is a type of fence that allows vines to crawl upwards. Life-size trellises are often found in rose gardens or supporting big clumps of honeysuckle. To make your own, gather eight twigs of equal length and get a glue gun ready. Lay four twigs horizontally, putting a drop of glue on each twig about a half inch apart. Then quickly, but carefully so as not to burn your fingers, place the other twigs vertically, making a grid. Plant some vinca or baby's tears and watch as they climb up your tiny trellis.

While you have twigs and a glue gun handy, you can also make a **fairy ladder,** which follows a similar pattern. Find two long sticks and then break another stick into about six pieces all roughly two inches in length. These are the rungs of your ladder. Glue the rungs across the side rails of the ladder until it is a desirable length.

Fairies are very tidy and, unlike most parents, love doing laundry. Making them a **clothesline** is a way to appeal to their sense of cleanliness. Simply tie a piece of twine between two twigs, making sure the line is at least six inches above the ground so fairy clothes don't drag on the dirt. Many stores carry miniature clothespins, which are cute as a button, but if you can't find these, use paperclips. Fairy clothes can be made by cutting leaves into the shape of a pair of pants or a dress and pinning them to the clothesline. An amazing book that has elaborate versions of fairy clothing is called *Fairie-ality: The Fashion Collection from the House of Ellwand* by David Ellwand.

To add festivity to any garden setting, use this same technique of stringing twine between two twigs, but instead of creating a clothesline, make a **fairy garland.** Cut triangles out of brightly colored felt and attach with a glue gun to your piece of twine. It will always look like a party is happening in your garden and knowing the fairies, one probably always is!

Garden Projects

4

When the winds of March are wakening the crocuses and crickets, did you ever find a fairy near some budding little thickets,...and when she sees you creeping up to get a closer peek, she tumbles through the daffodils, a-playing hide and seek.

~ MARJORIE BARROWS

BUTTERFLY GARDENS

The fairies are clapping their tiny hands and feverishly beating their wings because they are proud of you for making such stunning gardens. You can further enchant them by caring for their beloved friends, the butterflies and the birds. Butterflies help pollination by drinking the nectar deep inside a flower. Their mouth, also known as a proboscis, is like a long drinking straw sucking up delicious flower juice. While the butterfly drinks, pollen attaches to its body and is carried in flight to the other flowers, pollinating them and creating new flowers. Anyone who helps flowers this directly deserves the fairies' everlasting loyalty.

In order to pay tribute to all that these magnificent winged creatures do for the flowers, you can design and plant a garden just for them. Butterflies generally like many of the same flowers as fairies. But while a fairy has an entire language and history, as well as very specific uses for certain flowers, butterflies just tend to like the way flowers smell and their vivid colors. The kind of brilliant and dramatic flowers butterflies flock to require a sunny spot in the garden, but one also protected from harsh wind. Several of the plants that butterflies love are perennial (that word from earlier, meaning flowers that come back every year). Some of these include: yarrow, coreopsis, purple coneflower (also called echinacea), phlox, honeysuckle, columbine, and buddleia (also known as butterfly bush).

To attract that marathon migrator, the monarch, make sure to have some milkweed in your garden. Milkweed has a tendency to spread wildly due to the large number of seeds in its pods, so it is best to plant it in a more wild part of your yard. In the middle of the summer begin to look under the leaves of the milkweed and on its stalk for monarch caterpillars hungrily munching away. This is their main food source allowing them to fatten up in preparation for their miraculous journey.

BIRDS IN THE GARDEN

Hummingbirds will directly benefit from your work on a butterfly garden. The difference is that, while butterflies have a very good sense of smell, hummingbirds are solely attracted to color. Hummers love the color red and are particularly attracted to trumpet-shaped flowers. Honeysuckle, columbine, coral bells, sage, hibiscus, and petunias are all good choices for these tiny, lightning fast birds. You can also hang a hummingbird feeder on your porch and fill it with a sugar-water nectar.

Make sure that in your initial planning of your garden you create a place for a birdbath and a bird feeder. Birdbaths need not be complicated; a weatherproof basin mounted on a stump will work for a start. Keep the water fresh for the birds and you will really see them cleaning themselves. Birds and fairies, unlike some of you, actually like taking baths. There are many birdbath projects out there, several involving mosaic tiles. I have included one that takes a bit of doing but is quite amazing and sure to enchant a bird or a fairy into taking many baths. This is a true family project, so make sure you have your parents' blessing before you get your heart set on this. Any time you see Quick Crete in a project, be forewarned that a handsome mess will ensue.

Birdbaths and bird feeders show your goodwill to the fairies. Feeding birds is an all-year endeavor, but the birds really need your help in the winter. To prepare for

Recipe for a Birdbath

2 bags of Quick Crete

water

mounds of slightly damp sand

1 or 2 tarps

Saran Wrap

large rhubarb leaves

implements to pour, stir, and contain the quick-crete

1 Lay a tarp down, then make a large mound of sand on it.

2 Lay your rhubarb leaves over the sand mound covering the entire pile as best you can.

3 Mix your Quick Crete so that it is wet but firm.

4 Pour Quick Crete over the leaves in a thick layer, patting gently.

5 Cover your packed firm Quick Crete with Saran Wrap, so that the mix will not dry too quickly.

6 Cover your mound with a tarp and let dry for 1-2 weeks (dependent on weather).

this, collect a bare branch with several offshoots. Plant this in a large pot of dirt. Some people even pour concrete to make it really sturdy but I don't think this is necessary. Decorate your "tree" with all sorts of bird-treat ornaments. Suet balls wrapped in ribbon, peanut-butter-&-bird-seed pine cones, rose hips threaded with twine. Keep adding to your tree all winter and the birds will be well fed and delighted. A great book that complements this project is *Night Tree* by Eve Bunting, one of my absolute favorite winter books.

SCENT GARDENS

A scent garden is one that will entice you to take a snooze or sit and read your favorite books. There is nothing more agreeable than moving from plant to plant, gently releasing the essential oils and breathing them in. Because some of the plants in the scent category are quite vigorous spreaders, I suggest you make this garden in a large container or raised bed. The main culprit is mint, which is a huge traveler. Some of you might not mind mint's invasion, but I say it's better to be safe than smothered. There's a huge variety of mint to choose from, but chocolate mint is a must — it smells just like an Andes chocolate. For a lemony scent to complement the mint, try lemon verbena, lemon balm, or lemon grass. Scented geraniums come in many varieties such as rose, cinnamon, ginger, and nutmeg. Other great additions to the scent garden are lavender, thyme, and rosemary. Once you have planted and cared for your scented lovelies, clip the leaves and place them in the center of a bandana. Fold the bandana in half, then roll it up and wrap it around your wrist. All day long as the sachet meets your nose you will benefit from aromatherapy, the result of your hard work in the garden.

GARDEN FORTS

Perhaps you want a fort in the garden, a bigger version of the houses you built for the fairies. A place you can go to unwind and doze as the fairies do in all of the

special places you've created for them. Sure, you could curl up underneath a large fern or beneath a big patch of phlox, but creating your own garden fort is way more fun. One way is to make a teepee out of long sticks or bamboo, if you have access to it. The sticks should measure six to eight feet and be very straight. You will need at least fifteen poles. Start by pushing five of the poles into the ground in a circle, making sure you have a circumference of four to six feet. Cross the tops of the poles at the center of the circle, then tie them together with twine. Keep adding more poles equally around the circle, leaving a space for a door. When you have "planted" all of the poles, tie them all together at the top. Voilá, you have your teepee. Now plant some real climbers. Vitis, also known as grape vine, is a vigorous grower, as are sunflowers, morning glories, clematis, and moonflowers. Watch through the summer and your fort will soon be enveloped by green. If you are an impatient sort and desperate for some privacy, much like a fairy, you can cover the area around your fort with bark or weave thick grasses through the poles. Either way, by the end of summer you will have a green, unseen, privacy machine.

MUSIC AND LIGHT

You may think that we have covered it all. What else could you possibly do to your garden to make the fairies happier? Well, fairies love dancing. All of those dew tents you see early on summer mornings are remnants from fairy dance parties. So, in order for your fairy garden to be a true haven for those footloose fairies, you must provide a source of music. Wind chimes can be that source and are an overall

great addition to any garden. One family designated a tree in their backyard as a music tree. They bought steel pipes and drilled holes in the tops, hanging them from different heights. The kids gathered old pots and big spoons and hung them up as well. Look around your house to see if you have anything that might make music, but make sure to ask your parents before stringing up Great Aunt Alice's antique silver spoons!

While you are looking around for things that make music, search for items that create rainbows and dancing light. Fairies love prisms and reflected light. Making a mobile is a fun rainy-day project, and all you have to do to start is find two straight sticks about a foot long. Cross them and tie them together in the middle with a piece of wire, then tie a piece of string on each of the four corners. Old CDs, beads, sea glass, chandelier pendants, or even a single earring can be strung and added to your mobile. That's it! You have created a fairy garden wonderland. Butterflies and birds will flock to your garden. Music and light will permeate the neighborhood. Now is the time to celebrate and show off your garden.

5

Fairy Garden Tea Party

*"Leave room in your garden
for the fairies to dance."*

~ ANONYMOUS

You've worked really hard to create a remarkable garden and the fairies are eternally grateful. Now they plead with you to put your trowel down and have some fun. Since fairies love laughter and parties, what better way of christening your garden than with a fairy tea party?

61

INVITATIONS

Party planning can be elaborate or spur of the moment. Of course, a garden party does rely on the weather, so you should plan far in advance and make a rain date. Once you have an idea of when to have your party, make a list of friends to invite. Maybe you have friends who feel the same way about fairies as you do and will truly appreciate your hard work, or maybe you have some who just love eating cookies. No matter, make your list and get ready to create some **invitations**. An invitation can be as fancy or simple as you like. One idea is to cut paper into a tea-cup shape and write the invitation on that. Include a real tea bag of your favorite kind of tea for your friends to enjoy. You can also write your invitation on a hosta leaf in a gold pen and hand deliver the message. However you decide to create the invitation, make sure to put the time, date, rain date, location, and a phone number so people can let you know if they are coming.

PLANNING

Once all of your friends are invited, it's time to start planning. Tea parties need tea. And if you've planted herbs in your fairy garden this summer, you can make your own brew. Perhaps you have a mint patch or some chamomile or you've gathered some rose petals. If so, you have the fixings for a lovely herbal tea. If not, do not despair, as there are endless tea selections available at the store. Not everyone, particularly the very young, wants tea anyway, even at a tea party. So it is good to have juice or nectar on hand. To make it fairy friendly, you can create **fairy ice cubes**. At least a day before the party, sprinkle the petals from roses, nasturtiums, violets, clover, or berries into an ice cube tray. Then fill the tray with water and freeze. The day of the party, pull out the ice cubes to grace your guests' glasses.

Now for the **food**… a tea party would not be a tea party without some variety of **tea sandwiches**. Pull out your Christmas cookie cutters and a couple of loaves of bread. Cut out pairs of stars, hearts, flowers, anything but a Santa shape, then fill each pair of bread with some delicious sandwich fixing. I like cucumber and cream cheese. Your friends might like a simple peanut butter and jelly. If you make these ahead of time, cover them with a wet paper towel and Saran Wrap. They dry out very quickly.

If the party is in the afternoon, the guests will probably be in the mood for some serious sweets such as **marzipan toadstools**. Marzipan is an almond paste that is similar to Play-Doh. Divide ten ounces of almond paste into two sections and put one half in a small bowl. Add a few drops of red food coloring and mix with your hands, then break into eight pieces. Roll each piece of the red marzipan into a ball and then flatten into a toadstool shape. Next, take the uncolored marzipan and break off tiny little pieces to make spots on your mushrooms. Break the remaining chunk of marzipan into eight pieces and roll into mushroom-stalk shapes. Attach to the toadstool and arrange into a ring around a plate. You now have an edible fairy ring!

Since fairies value good health, it is important to serve your guests something with a few vitamins, and **fairy fruit wands** are the perfect solution. All you need are wooden skewers and a variety of fruit such as strawberries, melon, banana, grapes, and kiwi fruit. Cut them into bite-size pieces and stick them onto the skewer. For the magical star on the top of the wand, buy a star fruit and your guests will be wishing they never had to leave your party!

The beauty of a garden party is that the garden is the decoration. You can enhance the scenery by sewing a **garland** of blossoms threaded with a needle and string to festoon around your party area. A giant daisy or dandelion chain would also be festive. Place a big sheet or tablecloth in the center of your yard and set it with a vase of freshly picked flowers as well as your tea set. If you have a good idea who is coming, make some **place cards** so friends will know where they are sitting.

Having a few party activities keeps the flow going. A simple, fun activity is to have your guests make their own **fairy glitter gel**. All you need is aloe vera gel, fine glitter, and Dixie cups. If you want to be fancy you can find little lip gloss containers. Fill a cup about halfway with aloe and add a half-teaspoon of glitter. Stir and voilá, a shimmery gel for your cheeks and shoulders.

If your guests have a really good imagination — as I imagine they do since they are your friends — and they really enjoy playing outside, then, in addition to all of your lovely snacks and tea, have a mud-pie tea party. The mud-pie tea party

allows you to cook using nature's bounty for the fairies or dolls or even trolls. The premiere mud-pie party cookbook is called *Mud Pies and Other Recipes* by Marjorie Winslow. The contents include Appetizers, Soups, Salads and Sandwiches, Main Dishes, Pastries and Desserts, Beverages, and Suggested Menus. A great tea party recipe is for Boiled Buttons — "A hot soup that is simple but simply delicious. Place a handful of buttons in a saucepan half filled with water. Add a pinch of white sand and dust, 2 fruit-tree leaves, and a blade of grass for each button. Simmer on a hot rock for a few minutes to bring out the flavor. Ladle into bowls——." Also nice is Gravel en Casserole, Left-Handed Mudloaf, Pine Needle Upside Down Cake, and the infamous Pencil Sharpener Pudding.

As much fun as the mud-pie tea party can be, it will make a serious mess. After any party there is always a lot of clean-up. Remember the fairies love order and neatness? Your parents probably have a similar sensibility and if you hope to host many more parties in the future, I'd recommend enlisting your friends to help you do a clean sweep of the party grounds.

Indoor Projects

"Gentle fairies, hush your singing:
Can you hear my white bells ringing,
Ringing as from far away?
Who can tell me what they say?"

~ MARY CICELY BARKER

Maybe some of you live in a place where gardens stay green all year, and if so enjoy your bounty. But for those of us with long winters, don't despair. Your newly developed green thumb won't turn brown and wither. There are projects to keep you digging in the dirt even through the snowiest of days and ones to make the most of your summer harvest of flowers and herbs.

INDOOR FAIRY GARDENS

For those of you who made your fairy gardens in a container, you are in luck! Just bring that lovely display inside for the winter. Not all the plants you chose will last due to temperature or light changes, but jade plants or aloe will love the new inside condition. You can also add more delicate accessories since the weather won't be wreaking havoc on them. There is a vast list of plants that thrive indoors and will do very well in your fairy garden. Baby's tears, English ivy, ferns, and polka dot plants will all look lovely in your indoor garden. Watch your fairy garden throughout the winter and tend to it. Give it water, move things around, add new plants if space allows, and come spring you will know even more about gardening. And who knows, maybe the fairies will even come into your house to visit your garden.

PRESSED FLOWERS

Throughout the height of the blooming season, cut various flowers and leaves to press. Flat flowers such as pansies, black-eyed Susans, daisies, violets, and lavender are

the easiest to press. Make sure to cut the stems off as close to the flower head as possible. Place the flowers on wax paper and when you have filled the entire paper, cover with another sheet of wax paper. Place the sheets between the pages of a thick book. Pile several other heavy books on top. After two weeks, uncover the flowers and carefully remove them from the wax paper. Save these dried specimens for a cold winter day to create flowery bookmarks, stationery, and gift tags.

BULBS

Forcing bulbs is an activity that fills your house with the colors and fragrance of spring when it's still months away. Amaryllis and paperwhite narcissus need only a shallow bowl filled with pebbles or soil to hold the bulbs in place. Give them a drink and they will likely bloom about a month after you plant them. Buy a couple dozen paperwhite bulbs and store them in a cool, dry place. Start some every few weeks and they will bloom right through the winter.

POCKET PLOTS

Sprouts are another gratifying winter gardening option. Pocket Plots is an activity created by author Jane Bull in her book, *The Gardening Book.* A pocket plot is a tiny garden made in the lid of a peanut butter jar. First you fill the lid with a damp paper towel and then you gather some sprouting seeds such as mustard and cress. Place the seeds over about half of the lid, leaving the other areas for accessories. Cover the lid and keep the paper towel slightly wet. The sprouts will pop up very quickly and then you can add a tiny fairy and some colored rocks from an aquarium. These make great gifts and you can even eat the sprouts!

Winter is the perfect time for planning and dreaming about next year's garden. Ask your parents to order seed catalogs through the mail for you to pore over. Twigs will be abundant to make miniature garden furniture. And by the time the snow melts and the ground begins to soften, you will be ready to tackle another year in the garden. Each season will bring changes to the garden. You will probably make mistakes, innocent plants might die. You will get wet and dirty. But the landscape around you will be vibrant and humming with fairy energy. And if you fall in love with your garden, you will never lack for something to do ever again.

How to Know if Fairies Have Visited Your Garden?

"Buttercups in the sunshine look
like little cups of gold.
Perhaps the Faeries come to drink
the raindrops that they hold.

~ ELIZABETH T. DILLINGHAM, "A FAERY SONG"

In no time at all you have mastered the basics of fairy gardening. As each of your tiny seeds took root, the fairies took notice. The more you tended your garden bed, the more the fairies tended to you. I've probably said this a hundred times already, but the fairies love your garden and are no doubt helping you along. One surefire

way to tell if the fairies have visited is if the garden is lush and vibrant. If for some reason your garden hasn't taken off, don't despair, sometimes environmental factors like wind, heat, drought, or too much rain make it hard for even seasoned gardeners — and even fairies can't control the weather.

If you find that certain things disappear from your garden, like a trowel that you just set down, or a packet of seeds fresh from the garden store, maybe you have some mischievous elves, trolls, or even naughty fairies counteracting your efforts. To protect yourself in this event, there are very simple steps to take. First, wear your clothes inside out, then put a pinch of salt in your pocket, a red ribbon in your hair, a sock under your bed, and make a daisy chain. After doing all that you should be fine!

But back to the good stuff, whether those friendly, non-troublesome fairies are visiting you. This is where all of the patience you developed from watching seeds grow into plants comes in handy, because to see signs that fairies have visited you'll need to take the "long view." Taking the long view basically means knowing things might not happen right away.

But there are certain clues of fairy visitation to look out for. If you are ever in the garden and see out of the corner of your eye a flicker or a glimmer, almost like a firefly — if you see it and then you don't — well, that surely is a fairy. If you see a little globe, pearlescent perhaps, in the heart of a flower, that may be a baby flower fairy. Tinkling bells where there is no known source of music is another common sign. Many fairy seekers report seeing wind eddies or whirlwinds, or the bending of grass blades with no perceptible cause. Sometimes, the chills or goose bumps, or even a rise in the hair on the back of your neck may mean a fairy is nearby.

Some of you lucky few might one day even see a fairy ring. A fairy ring is a circle of mushrooms, stones, or grass that is taller than the rest of the grass. Just remember, do not step inside as you may be whisked away to fairyland with no chance of return. Dew tents, the little wispy canopies over the grass in the morning, are always a good sign that fairies have had fun the night before. And if you ever come across broken twigs arranged in patterns — that usually means a fairy is trying to tell you something. Pay attention!

Another sign of fairy presence is unexplainable losses of time, but childhood is filled with those and it might be hard to know when they are caused by fairies. I sure hope you lose track of time often, because that is when magic happens. Think of all those times when you are playing with your best friend after school and in what seems like five minutes your parents are there to pick you up. Talk about unexplainable losses of time!

The best sign of all that fairies have found your garden delightful is uncontrollable laughter. Side-splitting, deep-down, snorting, tear-inducing, pee-in-your-pants-by-accident — yeah, you know, that kind of laughter. The best kind. That is what the fairies will do to you if you are not careful! And that is what I wish for you as you garden — laughter and a sense of time slipping carelessly away as you tend to all the beauty around you. May your garden grow strong and your roots delve deep.

# Further Reading

Books on Gardening:

The Gardening Book by Jane Bull

Sunflower Houses by Sharon Lovejoy

Roots, Shoots, Buckets and Boots: Gardening Together with Children by Sharon Lovejoy

Dig, Plant, Grow: A Kid's Guide to Gardening by Felder Rushing

What Shall I Grow? by Ray Gibson

Gardening Projects for Kids by Jenny Hendy

Books on Fairies and Fairy Gardens:

Sweet Pea's Garden: Special Things to Make and Do Inspired by Cicely Mary Barker and written by Frederick Warne

Fairy Gardens: A Guide to Growing an Enchanting Miniature World by Betty Earl

The *Flower Fairy* series by Cicely Mary Barker

Fairy Garden: Fairies of the Four Seasons by Tom Cross and Constance Lewis

Mud Pies and Other Recipes by Marjorie Winslow

Fairie-ality: The Fashion Collection from the House of Ellwand and Fairie-ality: A Sourcebook of Inspirations from Nature by David Ellwand

The Real World of Fairies by Dora Van Gelder

Fairy Cooking by Rebecca Gilpin and Catherine Atkinson

Resources

Kerri Day at Mini Me
kerriday@fairpoint.net

Continental Collectables
flowerfairies.com

Market Hill
finefairyhouses.com

Gardener's Supply Company
gardeners.com

Shady Acres Herb Farm
shadyacres.com

Miniature Garden Shoppe
miniaturegardenshoppe.com

Enchanted Gardens
miniature-gardens.com

Enchanted World of Fairy Woodland
fairywoodland.com

Wee Trees
weetrees.com

Acknowledgements

Writing is very similar to gardening. Both require patience, hard work, and much variety. I feel so lucky to combine the two in this book and am thankful to Michael Steere for planting the idea of a gardening book and letting me 'fair-ify' it. Jen Smith-Mayo is a dream photographer with a true fairy eye, and Lynda Chilton made the book come alive. Thank you to Terry Brégy and Linda Callahan for taking the book to the street, Judy Paolini for sharing it with the world, and to everyone else at Down East who make the process fun and seamless.

Thank you to my writing group, Kathleen, Ari, Lacey, and Cree, for all of your good writing mojo, and especially to Ari for starting me on the fairy path.

Thank you to Sandy for sharing your magical fairy garden and introducing me to all the seers on your wiseacre!

I am grateful to the Rockport Public Library for the constant support, flexibility, and encouragement, especially to Molly Larson for putting up with my side job.

Thank you to Kerri Day and Lynn LeClair, who are the real deal in fairy gardening. The Coastal Maine Botanical Gardens, Hoboken Gardens, and Merryspring Gardens welcomed me into their beautiful facilities for my research and provide inspiring resources for our community.

Thank you to all my family and friends near and far for cheering me on in my fairy endeavors, and especially to my little crew. Jeff, the ship would surely sink without your calm and compassionate guidance. Phoebe, you are truly my best sounding board and editor, and Daphne, you are the embodiment of the fairy code. I love you all so much.